But Lord

A Scriptural Look at Popular Christian Beliefs

Jerry Graham, Ph.D., D.Min.

www.TheCoachingPair.com

JIREH Marketing, Inc.

Copyright Notice

First Printing, 2013

ISBN-13: 978-1492202806

ISBN-10: 1492202800

Printed in the United States of America

Table of Contents

Introduction:
But Lord, That Would
Mean I've Been Wrong

"Minds are like parachutes; they work best when open." (Lord Thomas Dewar [note that some attribute a minor variation of this quote to Frank Zappa.])

You and I definitely have an open mind—although I'm not always so sure about you. And like you, I can name hundreds of people who do not seem to be so blessed.

We as humans are convinced that we have an open mind about most things. But more and more research, as well as empirical evidence, demonstrates just the opposite. Just watch the nightly news for confirmation. Whether it's politics, religion, social programs, environmental issues, or any of hundreds of other issues, the inclination to hear other points of view seems to have evaporated. It even shows in which nightly news we watch—we avoid the channels that would expand our thinking in favor of those which further validate our positions.

As an aside, I believe most would have thought that the expansion of media-based information choices available to us would have had the effect of expanding our exposure to alternative points-of-view, but experience has shown just the opposite. The choices have morphed into niche markets drawing niche audiences with increasingly narrowly niched views.

Another of my favorite quotes is one by Anaïs Nin who said, "We don't see things as they are, we see them as we are." This suggests that we are all carrying around a load of baggage through which we view the world and perceive reality. That's scary stuff. That means that two people can witness the very same incident at the same time and then report, under oath, two very different accounts of what they saw.

This is not a new development by the way. It's more that we're just now beginning to understand the cognitive behavior of the human mind. There is a phenomenon called "inattentional blindness" which simply says that we are effectively blind to things that we are not paying attention to. In other words, one must focus their attention on something just to see it. In effect, looking is not seeing. There is a classic video demonstration of this that I encourage you to watch at http://youtu.be/IGQmdoK_ZfY.

(http://youtu.be/IGQmdoK_ZfY)

Stanford University psychologist Leon Festinger said, "A man with a conviction is a hard man to change. Tell him you disagree and he turns away. Show him facts or figures and he questions your sources. Appeal to logic and he fails to see your point." The real problem here is that we all have convictions. Some are conscious and some are buried deep in our subconscious mind. As Pontius Pilate asked Jesus in John 18:38, "What is truth?"

I personally had a head-on collision with this supposedly irrational behavior in the very recent past. I unequivocally fell into the category of Christians described by Wikipedia, "The predominant Christian view is that Jesus mediates a New Covenant relationship between God and his followers, according to the New Testament, which ended or set aside some or all of the Old Covenant. Christianity, almost without exception, teaches that this New Covenant is the instrument through which God offers mercy and atonement to mankind."

My thinking and theological mindset was challenged by some loving conversations with dear friends and further by some of the resources they offered to bolster their position. Since what they were proposing was at odds with my long-standing beliefs, I immediately (albeit unconsciously) began having thoughts that further calcified my position and helped me build arguments to challenge their obviously aberrant views.

As I look back on it, I have to confess that facts didn't seem to matter. There had to be some deep-seated pride in my being right that also was triggered by the on going encounters. To make matters worse, my wife was on their side. No matter the odds or the reasoning, it was clear that I was tenaciously holding on to my beliefs.

I'm not sure what caused the breakthrough. All I can surmise is the amazing power of the prayers of people who loved me. But the breakthrough did come. And the amazing thing is that when the breakthrough came, it came like a flood. I quickly forgot how close-minded I had been and began to wonder how so many other people could be so blind to the facts that I had been unwilling to hear. It's like the light had been turned on. I became a convert—and I have to confess that I'm glad I did.

This book is not my attempt to convert you, but to simply pose some interesting questions, accompanied by some inescapable facts (usually Scripture), in the hope that you too will stop long enough to question and evaluate the source of some of your beliefs.

With all that behind us, allow me to ask the first question. (BTW, the ideas behind most of these questions came from an amazing video presentation found at http://goo.gl/mwnti).

(http://goo.gl/mwnti)

Question One:
But Lord, Did
You Make a Mistake?

Why would God impose a Law on mankind in the first place if that Law was unkeepable and such a heavy burden that it oppressed mankind to the extent that He had to send His Son to repeal it? Is He sadistic? Did he make a mistake?

Unkeepable simply means not keepable. In other words, you can't keep it even if you wanted to. It is popularly believed that the reason we need Jesus is because no one could ever do everything the Old Testament (Torah) Law requires. What would a belief like that do to one's motivation to try to obey the Law?

Then add the opinion that the Law is such a heavy burden that it is oppressive. Oppressive is defined as burdensome, unjustly harsh, tyrannical, causing discomfort by being excessive, distressing, or grievous. Is this the same Law of which Moses wrote, "You shall therefore keep His statutes and His commandments which I command you today, that it may go well with you and with your children after you, and that you may prolong your days in the land which the LORD your God is giving you for all time?" (Deuteronomy 4:40) (Notice the phrase "for all time." What do you suppose that meant?)

Or about which David wrote, "The Law of the LORD is perfect, reviving the soul; the testimony of the LORD is sure, making wise the simple; the precepts of the LORD are right, rejoicing the heart; the commandment of the LORD is pure, enlightening the eyes; the fear of the LORD is clean, enduring forever; the rules of the LORD are true, and righteous altogether. More to be desired are they than gold, even much fine gold; sweeter also than honey and drippings of the honeycomb. Moreover, by them is your servant warned; in keeping them there is great reward?" (Psalm 19:7–11)

It seems that leaders who lived under the Old Testament Torah had a pretty different view of the Law than today's average Christian. Stop and consider—did God make a mistake when He instituted the Torah on His people? Was he being sadistic, i.e., did He derive pleasure in the cruelty of instituting a system of laws which He obviously knew His people couldn't keep? Is that the nature of the God you worship? Or did He, as perceived by Moses, David, et al. institute a system of laws designed to give people guidelines and instructions for living so that "all may go well with you?"

Did He really send His Son to repeal the Torah? How do you reconcile that belief with the statement made by Jesus in Matthew 5:17, "Do not think that I have come to abolish the Law or the Prophets; I have not come to abolish them but to fulfill them?" Then in the very next verse as He again says, "For assuredly, I say to you, till heaven and earth pass away, one jot or one tittle will by no means pass from the Law till all is fulfilled." Sounds a bit like the Law might just still be in place.

What do you think?

Question Two:
But Lord, Surely
You Don't Mean All

I f all scripture is instruction in righteousness, and if we are to practice righteousness, why do we think it is permissible to not practice all scripture?

Double talk? Not really. The very familiar passage of 2 Timothy 3:16–17 reads, "All Scripture is breathed out by God and profitable for teaching, for reproof, for correction, and for training in righteousness, that the man of God may be complete, equipped for every good work." Too often we conveniently forget the fact that when Paul wrote this letter to Timothy, the "all Scripture" he was referring to was what we call the Old Testament (which includes the Torah). The New Testament was not yet written or available to reference.

Therefore the "training in righteousness" that Paul speaks of is in large part from God's instruction manual, the Torah (which is better translated as direction, teaching, or instruction instead of Law). So what does that have to do with us today since as New

Testament Christians we are free from the Law. Or are we?

The New Testament book 1 John 2:3-6 reads, "And by this we know that we have come to know him, if we keep his commandments. Whoever says 'I know him' but does not keep his commandments is a liar, and the truth is not in him, but whoever keeps his word, in him truly the love of God is perfected. By this we may know that we are in him: whoever says he abides in him ought to walk in the same way in which he walked." Remember, the "commandments" John is referring to are found in the Torah, not in the New Testament.

1 John 3:7 reads, "Little children, let no one deceive you. Whoever practices righteousness is righteous, as he is righteous." Verse 10 reads, "By this it is evident who are the children of God, and who are the children of the devil: whoever does not practice righteousness is not of God, nor is the one who does not love his brother."

Now it should go without saying that the biblical use of righteousness means to follow the ways of God. Therefore, looking at those two books of the New Testament, it appears that it may not be a very wise choice to simply ignore the Torah.

Again, what do you think?

Question Three: But Lord, Were You Just Kidding?

I f God entered into a covenant with Abraham and his seed which God Himself declared to be an "everlasting covenant," when and how did that change to make room for a "new covenant?" Does that mean that other, purportedly everlasting covenants, such as the promise made to Noah is also subject to change? Could He change His mind on something we all consider fundamental to our faith, e.g., everlasting life?

The foundational and famous Abrahamic Covenant found in Genesis 17 reads in part, "And I will establish my covenant between me and you and your offspring after you throughout their generations for an everlasting covenant, to be God to you and to your offspring after you. And I will give to you and to your offspring after you the land of your sojournings, all the land of Canaan, for an everlasting possession, and I will be their God" (vss. 7–8).

Other famous covenants that God has entered into include the Noahic Covenant ("When the bow is in the clouds, I will see it and remember the everlasting covenant between God and every living creature of all flesh that is on the earth." Genesis 9:16), the Davidic Covenant ("For does not my house stand so with God? For he has made with me an everlasting covenant, ordered in all things and secure. For will he not cause to prosper all my help and my desire?" 2 Samuel 23:5), and the covenant with the land of Israel ("I will make a covenant of peace with them. It shall be an everlasting covenant with them. And I will set them in their land and multiply them, and will set my sanctuary in their midst forevermore." Ezekiel 37:26).

The difference between a covenant and a contract is profound. Contracts are what we today hire lawyers to make and break for us. They can be broken when one of the parties of the contract fail to keep their promises. Biblical covenants, on the other hand, put no conditions on being faithful. The commitment to love and serve is unconditional.

Therefore an everlasting covenant, especially one made by God and with God as one of the parties, is clearly a redundancy. The adjective "everlasting" is totally superfluous. Obviously, a covenant made by God is a God-sized promise that can be relied on. Remember, God does not lie (Numbers 23:19a—"God is not a man, so he does not lie," and Titus 1:2—"This truth gives them confidence that they have eternal life, which God—who does not lie—promised them before the world began"). Also, God does not change (Numbers 23:19b—"He is not human, so he does not change his mind.")

All that might suggest that what we so lovingly call the new covenant would be better called the renewed covenant. After all, a new something implies that the old something is now out of date and no longer functional. Given what we just reviewed, that would seem to be highly unlikely, if not totally impossible. (More about the notion of a "renewed covenant" in a later question.)

So it seems that the promise of eternal life that all we who are Christians so eagerly look forward to our whole lives and that is promised in that famous verse John 3:16, "For God so loved the world, that he gave his only Son, that whoever believes in him should not perish but have eternal life" is likely a pretty safe bet. He's not going to change His mind. Hallelujah!!

Isn't that reassuring?

Question Four:
But Lord, We've
Been Told That We're Free

S ince we are no longer under the Law, does that mean it is now permissible in God's eyes to steal, to commit adultery, to murder? Why not? How is that consistent with the notion that Jesus freed us from the Law?

I have to keep reminding myself that none (I pray) who calls themselves a Christian would ask such a question. But hopefully it will serve to highlight a few points that we should be willing to think about.

It seems that there are two fundamental presuppositions required to even ask such a question. First, that we have been freed from the Law. Second, that the Ten Commandments, is more of a burden to us and to mankind in general than a blessing.

Let's start with the second. Consider Deuteronomy 30:15–16 wherein God says, "See, I have set before you today life and good, death and evil. If you obey the commandments of the LORD your God that I command you today, by loving the LORD your God, by walking in his ways, and by keeping his commandments and his statutes and his rules, then you shall live and multiply, and the LORD your God will bless you in the land that you are entering to take possession of it." It seems rather clear from this quote that God designed the Torah, which includes the Ten Commandments, to be a blessing to mankind, life, and good—not a burden, death, and evil.

Yes, I suppose that there are times when the anger we feel would seem to justify murder or that the lust we feel would seem to justify adultery, but what kind of a world would it be if we felt no restraints, legal or otherwise, to hold our feelings in check. I don't think any rational human being would choose to live in a totally lawless society. I suppose it's kind of trite, but if we can view the Torah as a manufacturer's instruction manual, we should be able to see that the laws are there to make our lives better, not worse.

Now, let's return to the first presupposition, that Jesus freed us from the Law. Here are a couple of thoughts that might make you wonder whether or not what we've all been taught about Jesus really holds together under close examination.

There are any number of well-known Bible verses that demonstrate that God's Law is a gift that is sure and true, a blessing to all, perfect, freedom giving, holy, just, life-giving, light, and numerous other positive things. How could a Bible-believing Christian deny any of those attributes since Scripture backs them all? As we acknowledge and contemplate those incredible attributes, it seems that we should be more upset to be told that Christ's death took that amazing and wonderful gift away from us.

Secondly, think about that famous passage in Jeremiah 31:33, "For this is the covenant that I will make with the house of Israel after those days, declares the LORD: I will put my Law within them, and I will write it on their hearts. And I will be their God, and they shall be my people." Why would God bother to write His Law on mankind's hearts if His ultimate plan was to send His Son to die on the Cross just to abolish that Law? Does that make any sense at all?

One more—how do you reconcile Jesus' statement in Matthew 5:17–18 where he clearly says, "Do not think that I have come to abolish the Law or the Prophets; I have not come to abolish them but to fulfill them. For truly, I say to you, until heaven and earth pass away, not an iota, not a dot, will pass from the Law until all is accomplished?" Heaven and earth clearly have not passed away and all has not been accomplished until the end of the millennial reign of Christ is over. So how can the Law have been abolished for the believer?

Just a thought.

Question Five:
But Lord, Everyone
Knows That the Law
Is No Longer Relevant

What comes to your mind when you hear the word "Law"? Allow me to offer a couple English idioms using the word Law; "lay down the Law," and "letter of the Law," and "long arm of the Law" just to mention three. All pretty ominous sounding, wouldn't you agree?

Our culture used to have a great deal of respect for the Law, but it seems to have eroded over the last several decades. And it appears to be getting worse. The word "Law" has slowly evolved from having positive connotations to becoming very negative. People used to want to obey the Law because it was recognized that doing so contributed to the greater good, and the penalty for not doing so was feared. Today, it seems that a higher social premium is placed on how much you can get away with and not get caught.

Most of us are guilty. Think about driving down the Interstate. If you go the speed limit, you risk causing an accident because the flow of traffic is 5–10 mph faster and your speed causes people to have to change lanes or brake unexpectedly. It's generally accepted that you can go 5 mph over with total impunity. And it's more than just speeding—we're all pretty much looking for ways to "beat the system."

The same is true for Christians and our Bibles. Mention the word "Law" to the average Christian and you will likely hear phrases like, "we're free from the Law," "the Law has been done away with," "no one could keep the Law anyway," "legalism!" and many other phrases along those same lines of thought. The apparent disdain that our culture has for the Law seems to have leaked over into our churches. Although truth be told, the strong feelings against the Law of Moses or the Law of God goes way back to the early church Fathers who taught and believed that Jesus nailed the Law to the Cross (arising from a gross misunderstanding of Colossians 2:14).

The Hebrew word "Torah" is almost uniformly translated using the rather pejorative word "Law." A better translation of Torah would have been direction, teaching, or instruction. A recurring theme in the book of Deuteronomy alone makes the point repeatedly that the purpose for following the instructions (commands, statutes, regulations, i.e., Torah) from God on how to live yields positive results such as "all will be well" with them (Deuteronomy 4:40, 5:16, 6:3, 6:18, 12:25, 12:28, 22:7). It's very clear that God intended the Torah for good.

How can something that was originally given to be so positive have eroded to be perceived so negatively by the majority of believers? Do you suppose it has anything to do with the unfortunate word chosen by the translators—Law? How would you feel as a parent if the gift you had given your child was viewed with such scorn and contempt? Could it be that we have totally missed the proper understanding of the Torah?

Your thoughts?

Question Six:
But Lord, You Said
It Was Perfect, Then You
Changed It. I'm Confused.

O ne of the most memorable Bible verses from my early walk as a believer is Psalm 19:14 in which David writes, "Let the words of my mouth and the meditation of my heart be acceptable in your sight, O LORD, my rock and my redeemer." I believe one would be hard-pressed to find a Christian that would find that sentiment too "Old Testament" and not for today.

Earlier in that same Psalm, David wrote of the power of the heavens and earth to proclaim the glorious handiwork of God (vss. 1–6) and was even quoted by the Apostle Paul in Romans 10:18 as he declares, "Their voice has gone out to all the earth, and their words to the ends of the world."

But in the midst of all this social proof and acceptance of David's words, there are a few "troublesome" verses. They read, "The Law of the LORD is perfect, reviving the soul; the testimony of the LORD is sure, making wise the simple; the precepts of the LORD are right, rejoicing the heart; the commandment of the LORD is pure, enlightening the eyes; the fear of the LORD is clean, enduring forever; the rules of the LORD are true, and righteous altogether. More to be desired are they than gold, even much fine gold; sweeter also than honey and drippings of the honeycomb. Moreover, by them is your servant warned; in keeping them there is great reward." (vss. 7–11) Did David, or actually God speaking through David, get it wrong?

The Law of the LORD is perfect? Dictionary.com tells me that perfect means "excellent or complete beyond practical or theoretical improvement; entirely without any flaws, defects, or shortcomings; accurate, exact, or correct in every detail." How can it be that something that couldn't be improved had to be replaced by a new, improved version with the crucifixion of Jesus? If it had some flaws or shortcomings, it wouldn't have been declared to be perfect. Did God get it wrong? Or have we gotten it wrong in our understanding of what took place by the New Covenant?

But so many experts, theology scholars, including some of the original church fathers, all are in agreement that the Law was done away with at the Cross. How many expert testimonies does it take to overrule God's Word? Just asking.

Strikes me that we may be on some pretty dangerous ground with this one.

Note that it's not just quibbling over the perfectness of perfect—what about the testimony being sure, the precepts being right, the commandment being pure, the rules being true and righteous? I personally like the more desired than gold part as well as the sweeter than honey part, and especially the part about great reward from keeping them.

How about you? Thoughts?

Question Seven:
But Lord, You
Said Forever, Then You
Changed It. What's Next?

Sometimes it's fun to look closely at words. I've been thinking about "forever" a lot lately. Forever seems to be one of God's favorite words since he used it over 330 times in the Old Testament and around 50 times in the New Testament. God is the original long-term planner.

What exactly does forever mean? Well, my old friend Dictionary.com says, "without ever ending; eternally; to last forever; continually; incessantly; always; an endless or seemingly endless period of time." Just what I was expecting. No surprises there.

In spite of that, I believe most of us would agree that the definition of forever could be a variable, depending on who says it. For instance, forever to a politician might mean just until the election is over. The word forever to a lawyer might mean until we can get the contract changed. The word forever to a married couple might mean as long as they manage to stay in love. I think you get the idea.

But God is not a politician although His promises are too good to be true. God is not a lawyer although He provided an amazing set of laws (or a better word, instructions) all designed to make the circumstances of our lives go well for us and our children (Deuteronomy 4:40—"Therefore you shall keep his statutes and his commandments, which I command you today, that it may go well with you and with your children after you, and that you may prolong your days in the land that the LORD your God is giving you for all time"). God is a lover who has agape or an unconditional love for each of us no matter what we have done or ever will do. His love will never cease. It is forever.

But there does seem to be a slight glitch here. You see, God says the Sabbath is forever in Leviticus 16:31 ("It is a Sabbath of solemn rest to you, and you shall afflict yourselves; it is a statute forever"). In spite of that, very few Christians even observe the Sabbath. Oh, they believe, or have been told, that Sabbath for the Christian is on Sunday, but there seems to be no scriptural basis for that belief. The original intent was to be a day of rest, and yet for most Christians, Sunday is anything but a day of rest. Many look forward to Monday just to get some rest. Where's the forever part?

In 1 Chronicles 16:15, David commanded that the Asaph brothers sing a song of thanksgiving to the LORD proclaiming among other things that His covenant, the words He commanded, is forever for a thousand generations. Yet, most Christians are of the belief, or have been told, that the covenant changed at the Cross. Where's the forever in that?

Again in Psalm 119:160, the Psalmist writes, "The sum of your word is truth, and every one of your righteous rules endures forever." Yet, we have been told that the rules (or laws) were nailed to the Cross. Not very forever.

One last example—Isaiah 40:8 says, "The grass withers, the flower fades, but the word of our God will stand forever." Well some of His words anyway, for again we've been taught that there are a number of His words that are no longer for us today. What is it about forever that I am missing?

You know, this seems to be a pretty slippery slope. There are some parts of God's Word that we as believers rely on pretty heavily. One example that comes to mind is eternal life (John 3:16 plus forty some-odd other references). By it's very name, eternal life should mean life that lasts forever. Or is that subject to change as well? Of course, I'm kidding—I hope.

What about you? How forever is forever to you?

Question Eight:
But Lord, I Thought
You Changed All That

Deuteronomy 10:12–13 reads, "And now, Israel, what does the LORD your God require of you, but to fear the LORD your God, to walk in all his ways, to love him, to serve the LORD your God with all your heart and with all your soul, and to keep the commandments and statutes of the LORD, which I am commanding you today for your good?"

Most Christians would quickly agree that they "fear the LORD" and many would say they try "to walk in all his ways (but we must remember, it's impossible to keep all the laws, so therefore we seem to feel free to pick the ones we can keep and ignore the rest).

When it comes "to love him" most would shout "Absolutely!!!" "Serve the LORD...with all your heart...and soul" would again elicit a hearty "Absolutely!" from a large proportion of Christians—after all they serve the church in this area or that, they teach

Sunday School, volunteer in the nursery, spend major blocks of time at the church, etc.

But then we come to "keep the commandments and statues of the LORD" and our crowd thins out pretty rapidly. Again, we can't possibly keep them all because they're just too hard, and remember, Jesus came to free us of that burden anyway. Hallelujah!!!

Given the above logic, isn't it interesting when we work our way over to 1 John 2:5–6 and read, "but whoever keeps his word, in him truly the love of God is perfected. By this we may know that we are in him: whoever says he abides in him ought to walk in the same way in which he walked." We run right into that pesky clause "whoever keeps his word." Could that mean all his word? Surely not. Then it says, "ought to walk in the same way in which he walked." But Jesus was sinless and perfect! How can we possibly walk in the same way he walked?

What about the verse back in Matthew 5 in which Jesus says, "Do not think that I have come to abolish the Law or the Prophets; I have not come to abolish them but to fulfill them?" What are we going to do with that?

To make matters worse, what about Paul's admonition in 1 Corinthians 11:1 in when he says, "Be imitators of me, as I am of Christ." Even Paul is saying we should follow Christ's example. How can that be? He is saying in so many words that he (Paul) imitated Jesus and that we should imitate Paul in that regard. Where does that done away with part fit into all this?

It's interesting to note that a careful reading of the New Testament reveals that Jesus was totally Torah observant. He was totally Jewish, observed the Jewish Sabbath (from sunset Friday to sunset Saturday), observed all the Jewish laws found in the Torah (although frequently accused otherwise), observed all the Jewish festivals, etc.

It is interesting also to note that a careful reading of Acts and the Pauline epistles reveals that Paul did likewise. Just as he said, he imitated Christ.

But I thought the laws were eliminated at the Cross. Apparently not—or at least according to Paul's example for which he admonished us to follow his lead.

Are you seeing the inconsistencies in all this? Seems that some of what we've been taught all these years just doesn't quite line up with the Scriptures.

Raises some interesting questions, don't you think? How do you resolve those apparent inconsistencies?

Question Nine:
But Lord, Didn't Paul
Say the Law Was a Curse?

Did Paul really say the Law (Torah) was a curse? This allegation comes from Galatians 3:10 and 3:13. In the former, he writes, "For all who rely on works of the Law are under a curse; for it is written, 'Cursed be everyone who does not abide by all things written in the Book of the Law, and do them.'" In the latter Paul says, "Christ redeemed us from the curse of the Law by becoming a curse for us—for it is written, 'Cursed is everyone who is hanged on a tree.'"

First of all, let's remember that Peter warned us that Paul's letters are hard to understand. He further warned us in 2 Peter 3:16–17 that "There are some things in them that are hard to understand, which the ignorant and unstable twist to their own destruction, as they do the other Scriptures. You therefore, beloved, knowing this beforehand, take care that you are not carried away with the error of lawless people and lose your own stability." That warning alone should cause us to take a second look at what Paul has written in those verses in Galatians.

Careful inspection shows that he is not really calling the Law a curse, but instead is saying that those who "rely on works of the Law [for salvation] are under a curse." The New Living Translation of this verse is perhaps the clearest as it reads, "But those who depend on the Law to make them right with God are under his curse..." So Paul is merely saying that those who rely on their works instead of faith to get right with God are under the curse of the Law found back in Deuteronomy 27:26. When you get a minute, look up the Galatians verses in the King James version that is still one of the most popular translations. You'll find that coming away with the notion that Paul is calling the Law a curse is pretty easy to do with that rendering.

So it should be clear that the use of the word curse by Paul in Galatians is referring to the curse that is clearly spelled out back in Deuteronomy, and he is by no means calling the Law itself a curse. The curse is simply a provision of the Law that speaks to non-compliance.

To further dispel the idea that Paul thinks the Law is a curse, look at Romans 7:12 where he says the Law is "holy and righteous and good." Again in Romans 7:14, Paul says the Law is "spiritual." And then in vs. 22 he says that he "delights in the Law of God." Doesn't sound like someone who believes the Law is a curse, does it?

Finally, look at Acts 21:21–26 and read where Paul is agreeing to an action designed to successfully dispel the widespread accusation against him that he has been teaching "all the Jews who are among the Gentiles to forsake Moses, telling them not to circumcise their children or walk according to our customs."

A curse? Hardly! Sounds like some self-serving scripture "twisting" by some "ignorant and unstable" folks trying to sell an agenda. Thank you Peter, for the heads up on this one.

As an aside, it's curious to me as to why Christians are so quick to remember the curse part of these verses. Any ideas?

Question Ten:
But Lord, Everybody Tells Me That We're Not Under the Law Anymore

This is a very common question for Christians to ask. Most have been told all their Christian lives that Jesus came to do away with the Law, and that as Christians, we are no longer under the Law.

First of all, what does not being under the Law mean? Does it mean that you can do anything you want because the Law doesn't apply to you? (This is very similar to the issue addressed in Question Four.) It's hard to imagine that a Christian would even remotely think that they are above the Law.

Put this in the context of our American traffic laws. When you stop at a stop sign or a red light, do you do that because you are under the Law? No, you do that simply because you are a Law-abiding citizen who is being legal—not legalistic! Now, if you chose not to stop and a traffic cop pulled you over, you may have to pay a fine for not stopping, and at that point you could reasonably argue that you were under the Law for that breech of a traffic regulation.

But through all that, you hopefully recognize the wisdom behind having traffic laws, and other than the fact that you were caught breaking one of them, a little reflection should result in a feeling of gratitude for the laws. Can you imagine living in a society where there were no traffic laws? The chaos would be absolutely unbelievable.

So, back to the issue at hand, is it acceptable to say that as a Christian you are not under the Law because Jesus died to pay the penalty for any breeches of the Law that you may make, past or future? Of course it is because that is a perfectly accurate statement. But that doesn't mean you have the right to be lawless. It doesn't mean you can do anything you want to do.

In fact, as a Christian, you are grateful for the laws because they provide definitive guidelines regarding how to please God. You recognize that God made those laws (Torah) for your benefit, and that following them to the best of your ability is life giving. In fact, you are so grateful for the laws and for Jesus paying your penalty for any and all breaches of the Law that you find yourself literally bending over backwards to observe them just to please God.

And amazingly, you find that the Holy Spirit not only reminds you of the laws, but He also provides you with the power (and the "want to") to keep the laws.

So in final analysis, you don't observe the laws because you are under the Law (perceived as a negative thing), but you observe the laws simply because you want to please God. And since the Holy Spirit is helping you, keeping the laws most certainly is not a burden. It is, in fact, a joy!

Such a deal!!!

Oh, by the way, regarding that myth that Jesus came to do away with the Law, I invite you once again to consider the fact that if Jesus truly came to do away with the Law as many believe, why would God want to write it on our hearts according to Jeremiah 31:31 and Hebrews 8:8ff.

By the way again, if the Law were truly as bad as many make it out to be, why would a loving God want to write it on our hearts in the first place? Does that make any sense to you? Could it be that we have been misinformed about the Law all these years? Just asking.

What do you think?

Question Eleven:
But Lord, Don't
We Live In the Age of
Grace Rather Than Law?

How many times have you heard someone in spiritual authority teach that we are so blessed to be living in New Testament times because we can be saved by grace whereas those unfortunate enough to live back in the Old Testament days had to be saved by keeping the Law.

Seems reasonable—until you recall the story of David and Bathsheba and find yourself wondering if David was saved. He certainly broke the Law. What about his son, Solomon? How many laws did he break?

But the real question comes up when you come across Numbers 23:19 (God is not man, that he should lie, or a son of man, that he should change his mind. Has he said, and will he not do it? Or has he spoken, and will he not fulfill it?). Or how about Hebrews 13:8 (Jesus Christ is the same yesterday and today and forever)?

If God didn't or doesn't change, how can we have one legal system for one period of time and then another for another period of time? Does that make any sense to you? Well, it shouldn't because it's just not logical.

God is a god of love and grace and has been so since time began. Grace was very much alive in the Old Testament. For the skeptic, I invite you to do a Google search using the argument "grace in the old testament" and read some of the articles you will find there. You see, the Old Testament was based on love, not fear. It was religion that turned that love into fear.

The Old Testament is replete with examples of people (and nations) that were on the receiving end of God's grace. A partial list includes Enoch, Noah, Abraham, Sarah, Isaac, Jacob, Joseph, Moses, Ruth the Moabitess, the children of Israel, the evil and feared Ninevites, Hannah the mother of Samuel, David, and even the ungodly kings Ahab and Manasseh.

Yes, we are certainly blessed to be living this side of the Cross, because we have the example of the "Living Torah" to guide our lives and redeem us from our sins. Plus, we have the Torah laws written on our hearts. And finally, we have the Holy Spirit to give us the desire and ability to live our lives according to the Torah.

Yes, we are saved by grace, but then again, so were Abraham (Romans 4) and all the other Old Testament figures we have read about.

But the fact that we have been saved by grace does not give us the license to live lawless lives. As Paul so famously said, "May it never be!"

Question Twelve:
But Lord, I Thought
Paul Taught That the
Law Was For the Jews Only

T his is an amazing misconception that the majority of the Christian church has to this day. What makes it so fascinating is that Peter saw it coming and specifically warned against it in his letter. He wrote, "And remember, our Lord's patience gives people time to be saved. This is what our beloved brother Paul also wrote to you with the wisdom God gave him—speaking of these things in all of his letters. Some of his comments are hard to understand, and those who are ignorant and unstable have twisted his letters to mean something quite different, just as they do with other parts of Scripture. And this will result in their destruction. I am warning you ahead of time, dear friends. Be on guard so that you will not be carried away by the errors of these wicked people and lose your own secure footing." (2 Peter 3:15–17)

You see, even though Paul was officially named as an Apostle to the Gentiles (Romans 11:13b—"God has appointed me as the apostle to the Gentiles"), he was still very much a Jew. He never considered himself a "Christian." Yes, he was affiliated with the sect of Judaism known as the Way which meant, among other things, that he recognized Jesus as the Messiah. But at the end of the day, Paul was a Jew, a Pharisee of the Pharisees, and of the tribe of Benjamin. One of the reasons we misunderstand him is because we read his writing through the lens and understanding of a Western Christian (which Paul wasn't) rather than through the lens of a rabbinically trained Jewish Pharisee (which Paul was).

A couple of key verses from Acts attest to Paul's lifelong commitment to the Torah:

- Acts 22:3—"Then Paul said, 'I am a Jew, born in Tarsus, a city in Cilicia, and I was brought up and educated here in Jerusalem under Gamaliel. As his student, I was carefully trained in our Jewish laws and customs. I became very zealous to honor God in everything I did, just like all of you today.'"
- Acts 23:6—"Paul realized that some members of the high council were Sadducees and some were Pharisees, so he shouted, 'Brothers, I am a Pharisee, as were my ancestors! And I am on trial because my hope is in the resurrection of the dead!'"
- Acts 24:14—"But I admit that I follow the Way, which they call a cult. I worship the God of our

ancestors, and I firmly believe the Jewish Law and everything written in the prophets."

- And perhaps most importantly, Acts 28:17–18— "Three days after Paul's arrival, he called together the local Jewish leaders. He said to them, 'Brothers, I was arrested in Jerusalem and handed over to the Roman government, even though I had done nothing against our people or the customs of our ancestors. The Romans tried me and wanted to release me, because they found no cause for the death sentence.'"

All this to say that Paul would never dream of turning his back on keeping the Jewish Sabbath, attending weekly synagogue services, observing all the Jewish appointed times or holidays, and most certainly would never knowingly violate any aspect of the Torah Law nor encourage his gentile constituency to violate the Torah. Yet in spite of this well-documented commitment to Jewish laws and traditions, it is commonly taught from pulpits today that Paul taught that the Law was burdensome, confining, and "nailed to the Cross."

Talk about being misunderstood! Again, a reminder of Peter's warning—"I am warning you ahead of time, dear friends. Be on guard so that you will not be carried away by the errors of these wicked people and lose your own secure footing." Losing that secure footing as he puts it, will ultimately "result in your destruction."

Ouch!!!

Question Thirteen: But Lord, Didn't Jesus Come To Do Away With the Law?

nother very powerful and pervasive myth in today's Christian church is the idea that Jesus was constantly at odds with the religious leaders of his day and that he kept "chipping away" at the Law as they were presenting it until His final act on earth was to nail the Law to the Cross ushering in the Age of Grace.

We addressed the Age of Grace in Question Eleven, so we won't rehash that here. Instead, we'll focus on the attitude of Christ toward the Torah during His earthly ministry. First, let's deal with the idea of nailing the Law to the Cross. This thought undoubtedly arises from Colossians 2:14 which reads, "Blotting out the handwriting of ordinances that was against us, which was contrary to us, and took it out of the way, nailing it to his cross." Just seeing the words "ordinances" and "nailing it to the Cross" in the same verse make it an extraordinarily logical leap to the misunderstanding that the ordinances (laws) were nailed to His Cross.

However, a closer reading of that verse and especially looking at other translations make it clear that it was our violations or breeches of the Law that got nailed to the Cross, not the Law itself. The Law is still very much in existence.

But since Jesus took upon Himself our penalty for our sins, it makes much more sense to see that it was the charges against us (and the subsequent penalties) that were nailed to the Cross. The New Living Translation verifies that interpretation—"He canceled the record of the charges against us and took it away by nailing it to the cross."

That aside, now let's go back to the beginning of this issue. First of all, Jesus was a Jew, born into a Jewish family. He faithfully attended synagogue (on Saturdays I might add), celebrated Hanukkah as well as all the other Jewish festivals. His close followers were Jewish. He came to seek the lost sheep of Israel (Matthew 15:24). Jesus lived His life in total and perfect compliance with the Torah and was even widely acknowledged as a teacher (rabbi, a term of honor and respect) of the Torah. He certainly died as a Jew.

The repeated conflicts Jesus had with the religious leaders of His day were never over issues within the Torah but were always about extensions to the Torah put in place by the often overzealous Jewish hierarchy. These extensions to the Torah were known as the oral Law as opposed to the written Law as received by Moses. You may recall that God, as He gave the

Law, ordered, "And now, O Israel, listen to the statutes and the rules that I am teaching you, and do them, that you may live, and go in and take possession of the land that the LORD, the God of your fathers, is giving you. You shall not add to the word that I command you, nor take from it, that you may keep the commandments of the LORD your God that I command you" (Deuteronomy 4:1–2).

In every case where it appears that Jesus is challenging the Pharisees and Sadducees over some issue of the Law, a closer look reveals that it is over an issue that is a variation of the Torah and not the Torah itself. The Law as given was perfect (Psalm 19:7) and you cannot further perfect perfection. Again, Jesus was 100% Torah observant, and therefore perfect in His compliance with the Law. Otherwise His death as the perfect, unblemished lamb would have been a total sham.

Finally, one has to wonder how the idea that Jesus did away with the Law at the Cross continues to have legs in view of the rather succinct disclaimer He gives in Matthew 5:17–19 wherein he says, "Do not think that I have come to abolish the Law or the Prophets; I have not come to abolish them but to fulfill them. For truly, I say to you, until heaven and earth pass away, not an iota, not a dot, will pass from the Law until all is accomplished. Therefore whoever relaxes one of the least of these commandments and teaches others to do the same will be called least in the kingdom of heaven, but whoever does them and teaches them will be called great in the kingdom of heaven."

Perhaps the confusion comes from the word "fulfill." But no matter how you slice it, it's impossible to interpret fulfill as eliminate. When you fulfill something you don't eliminate it.

Or fulfill could be interpreted as I have come to give you a model of living the laws fully or in their totality. The Complete Jewish Bible uses the word "complete" for fulfill. The New Living Translation uses "accomplish their purpose."

The point is, there just doesn't seem to be any scriptural justification for believing that Jesus did away with the Law or the Torah.

What do you think?

Question Fourteen: But Lord, Didn't You Say That All Foods Are OK?

This perception comes from Mark 7:18–19 ("And he said to them, 'Then are you also without understanding? Do you not see that whatever goes into a person from outside cannot defile him, since it enters not his heart but his stomach, and is expelled'"). Many translations then add parenthetically "(Thus He declared all foods clean.)"

Notice the shift from a narrative style of reporting of Jesus' words to a parenthetical statement which is clearly an editorial addition made by Mark, presumably to add clarity. So, it is technically incorrect to make the statement that Jesus said that all foods are clean. Mark is the one who said that.

But, that's a rather small point in this discussion. The larger point revolves around the word "food." The Greek word *broma* translated as "food" is defined by Strong's Lexicon as "that which is eaten, food."

To understand the significance of that, let me offer an example. Let's say you're my houseguest, and I encourage you to make yourself at home, and if you get hungry, feel free to eat any food you find in the house. I leave to run an errand, and come home to find that you've cooked my dog and my cat, and are slicing up my drapes to put in a stew. Now that's admittedly a ridiculous example, because you and I would obviously have a fairly common understanding of the word "food," and dogs, cats, and drapes are definitely not included.

One of the basic rules of biblical hermeneutics is that you must understand the context of the passage, who is doing the talking/writing, who is the audience, where are those in the audience from, and what do they believe. For our case here, it is sufficient to note that Jesus is talking to His disciples, and of course both Jesus and His disciples are Torah observant Jews.

To those who had spent their entire lives living in a highly religious culture among the Jewish people, their definition of food is unambiguously defined in the Torah (see Leviticus 11). The list of acceptable foods is well understood, and if something is not on that list it is not food and there is no question about it. So you can bet with total certainty that the disciples didn't race out and order ham sandwiches after this little teaching from their Master which was reported by Mark.

So here again, we see that Jesus was not changing or rewriting the Torah to eliminate the dietary laws established by God through Moses. And clearly the disciples and any of the Pharisees hanging around didn't take it that He had, or the uproar would have been immediate. After all, the dietary laws where one of the fundamental distinctives of the Jewish culture.

And I might add, the dietary laws given by God were not given maliciously to deprive us of tasty food. Au contraire! Like all the instructions given by God, they were given to make our lives better and more successful. They were for our benefit. For example, with regards to eating pork and shellfish, there is an abundance of scientific evidence to show that those "foods" are not the best choice from a health standpoint. But that's a topic for another day.

Question Fifteen:
But Lord, Why Do You
Give and Then Take Away?

There is a very popular Christian song called "Blessed Be Your Name" that contains the following lyrics:

> You give and take away,
> You give and take away,
> My heart will choose to say,
> Lord, Blessed be Your name.

It all sounds so very noble, but it creates an unfortunate and incorrect perception of a God who gives a blessing and then arbitrarily and at any moment, can capriciously choose to take it away for no apparent reason. That perception doesn't exactly promote a wholehearted trust in God.

Of course this is biblical they argue. It's virtually a direct quote from the Bible. Job, the oldest book in the Bible, closes the first chapter with, "And he said, 'Naked I came from my mother's womb, and naked shall I return. The LORD gave, and the LORD

has taken away; blessed be the name of the LORD.'
In all this Job did not sin or charge God with wrong"
(Job 1:21–22).

This was Job's cry when he received the horrible news that his seven sons and three daughters had been killed in an amazing set of circumstances wherein he also lost his health, his wealth, and his servants. This story and quote from Job has been used for years to explain the unexplainable when bad things happen to good people. It is the basis of a theology that paints God in a very unflattering and dubious light. But it's in the Bible, so it must be true. Right?

This blaming of God for unexplainable bad things spills over into our society and is widely accepted as the explanation for those bad things. For example, almost all insurance companies refer to natural disasters as "acts of God." If, as is the case for so many in our post-Christian culture, the only time you hear references to God is in association with catastrophe, e.g., hurricanes, tornados, fires, premature death, etc., you certainly come away with a fairly warped picture of God. Add to that the poor image of fathers that so many hold in our "fatherless" culture, and it is little wonder that Christianity has become more and more irrelevant to a growing population.

The problem with all this is that at the end of the book of Job (a very long book filled with the humanistically misguided opinions of Job and his friends), Job goes on to admit that his initial blaming of God for his tragic loss was totally incorrect.

Job 42:6 reads, "I take back everything I said, and I sit in dust and ashes to show my repentance."

The amazing thing to me is that the world is so quick to remember Job 1:21 and then totally forget (or more likely, be totally unaware of) Job 42:6. In essence, what Job admitted to be words spoken without knowledge are being repeated today as if they were sound theology. Doesn't this whole scenario remind you of the original attack on God's character and motives that Satan sold Eve in the Garden (Genesis 3:4-5)?

This, like all the preceding chapters, is yet one more example of how quickly we adopt the theology that others, usually with all good intentions, have taught us. We then make decisions through the rest of our lives from the basis of those misinformed beliefs that could so easily be dispelled by just reading our Bibles with an open mind. Personally, I purpose to be a little more careful and deliberate about what I allow others to inject into my thinking.

How about you?

Epilogue:
But Lord, There
Are So Many Questions

S o far, I've listed and commented on only 15 questions, which I believe we should all be willing to research and answer for ourselves. They are issues where the conventional wisdom and traditional teaching seems to leave us with more questions than answers. As you might expect, there are lots more questions just like these 15 that beg for answers.

Hopefully you did not feel any pressure from me to agree with my analyses nor my answers. After all, the theme of this whole book is that we've all been far too gullible in our accepting without question those things presented to us by our friends and by those we have chosen to look to as spiritual authorities. The only way to rise above that concern is to do our own research. After all, all it takes is a Bible.

As a way of drawing this book to a close, I am

going to leave you with a long, unordered list of questions that still need answers. Some of the questions are from the source I quoted in the Introduction, i.e., http://goo.gl/mwnti. Many, if not most, are questions that have come to me in the course of researching the answers I have presented in this book.

Enjoy your search!

- James 1:25 tells us that the Law of God is freedom ("But whoever looks intently into the perfect Law that gives freedom, and continues in it—not forgetting what they have heard, but doing it—they will be blessed in what they do"). And Psalm 119: 44–45 reads, "So shall I keep thy Law continually for ever and ever. And I will walk at liberty: for I seek thy precepts." How then can we say that the source of freedom and liberty is bondage?

- Proverbs 2:20 reads, "So you may walk in the way of goodness, and keep to the paths of righteousness." Isaiah 51:7a says, "Listen to Me, you who know righteousness, You people in whose heart is My Law." (See also Psalm 119:142; Deuteronomy 4:8; 2 Peter 2:21.) Since some say that the Law was changed, does that mean that the ways of righteousness were changed as well? Indeed, is it even possible for the ways of righteousness to change?

- Psalm 119:142 clearly states that the Law of God is true ("Your righteousness is righteous forever, and Your Law is true"). How can the Law of God that has been declared to be true, now not be true?

- Psalm 119:1 asserts, "Blessed are those whose ways are blameless, who walk according to the Law of the LORD." (Similarly see Exodus 18:20; Deuteronomy 10:12; 1 Kings 2:3; Proverbs 6:23; Isaiah 2:3; Malachi 2:8; Mark 12:14.) In view of those Scriptures, can the Way of God become a different way?

- "Everyone who sins is breaking God's Law, for all sin is contrary to the Law of God" according to 1 John 3:4. If breaking the Law of God is sin, can what is defined as sin suddenly become OK? Can the definition of sin be changed?

- According to Psalm 119:105–106 the Law of God is light ("Your word is a lamp for my feet, a light on my path. I have taken an oath and confirmed it, that I will follow your righteous laws"). That being the case, can light stop being light?

- If the Law of God is life ("Blessed are those who do His commandments, that they may have the right to the tree of life and may enter through the gates into the city." Revelation 22:14), can what is life no longer be life?

- If God is the Word (John 1:1) and God does not change (Malachi 3:6), how can we say the Word changed?

- We are told over and over that we are to delight in the Law (Psalm 1:2—"But His delight is in the Law of the LORD") and that the "Law is my [our] delight" (Psalm 119:70, 77, 92, 174; Romans 7:22). Doesn't it make you wonder when the Law stopped being a delight?

- According to John 1:14, Christ is the Word in the flesh. Then according to Revelation 19:13, Christ is the Word of God. Many believe and teach that significant portions of the Word of God have now been abolished. The logical question that then must be answered becomes, Did Christ abolish part of Himself?"

- Building on the previous question, if Jesus Christ, our Savior is the Word of God (Revelation 19:13), and Hebrews 13:8 assures us that He is the same yesterday, today, and forever, how then can we logically agree with those who insist that the Word of God changed?

- Jesus summarized all the commandments in Matthew 22:35–40 as He said, "You shall love the LORD your God with all your heart, with all your soul, and with all your mind. This is the first and great commandment. And the second is like it: You shall love your neighbor as yourself. On these commandments hang all the Law and the Prophets." Therefore, if the Law of God is how we are to love, and if the Law of God has been abolished, does that mean that the way we love God and others changes as well?

- A repetitive theme throughout the whole Bible is that the Law was intended to be good for us and to bless us (e.g., Deuteronomy 11:26–27; Psalm 112:1; Psalm 119; Psalm 128:1; Isaiah 56:2; Matthew 5:6, 10; Luke 11:28; James 1:25; 1 Peter 3:14; Revelation 22:14). Does it then make any sense at all for God to take the Law away from us after the Cross?

- Keeping all of God's commandments is the whole duty of man according to Ecclesiastes 12:13 ("Now all has been heard; here is the conclusion of the matter; Fear God and keep His commandments, for this is the duty of all mankind.") Does it not strain credibility to think that this is no longer true? If that were the case, what is the new, improved "whole duty of man?"

- If it is true that the Law cannot change till heaven and earth passes away as Jesus claimed in Matthew 5:17–18, and if it is also true that anyone who teaches that the Law changed will be least in the Kingdom (Matthew 5:19), why is it so widely taught in churches throughout the land that the Law of God changed when Jesus died on the Cross? Or did heaven and earth pass away and some of us just missed it?

- When Christ told His followers to "observe and do" what is taught from Moses' seat (Matthew 23:1–3), and given the understanding that what was taught from Moses seat was the Law of God as recorded by Moses, why do so many of His present day followers refuse to do what He said?

- Paul claimed that he taught and practiced what Moses wrote (i.e., the Law—Acts 21:20–26; 24:13–14; 25:8) and yet so many insist that he taught that the Law was bondage and not for the Gentile believers. What is the scriptural basis for that claim? Paul further taught that there was no difference between Jew and Greek (1 Corinthians 12:12–14; Galatians 3:27–29; Colossians 3:10–12). Therefore, how can we be comfortable using Paul's letters to teach that we do not have to observe all of God's Law? How is Paul both against the Law and for the Law?

- In Romans 3:31 Paul wrote, "Do we then overthrow the Law by this faith? By no means! On the contrary, we uphold the Law." By that it is clear that he is teaching that the Law of God is not void and that we are to continue in the Law. Have you ever wondered why we continue to teach differently? (And blame it on Paul?)

- Moses wrote, "There is to be one Law and one ordinance for you and for the alien [Gentile] who sojourns with you" (Numbers 15:16; Exodus 12:19, 38, 49; Leviticus 19:34, 24:22; Numbers 9:14, 15:15–16, 29). Since Paul practiced and taught Moses, then that means he had to teach it to converted Gentiles. Isn't it curious that there are still accusations against Paul that he taught against the Law of Moses? What (or who) is behind all this misinformation?

- If we are to love God by keeping His commandments (1 John 5:2–3) as a response to His loving us (1 John 4:19), why do we feel we only need to keep some of His commandments? (Like the one's we choose to keep.)

- In the context of the LORD's return, Isaiah says, "See, the LORD is coming with fire, and his chariots are like a whirlwind; he will bring down his anger with fury, and his rebuke with flames of fire. For with fire and with his sword the LORD will execute judgment on all people, and many will be those slain by the LORD. 'Those who consecrate and purify themselves to go into the gardens, following one who is among those who eat the flesh of pigs, rats, and other unclean things—they will meet their end together with the one they follow,' declares the LORD" (Isaiah 66:15–17). Doesn't that make you ask yourself the question, "If He will care at that point in the future, why do we assume that He doesn't care now?"

- Zechariah prophesied (14:16), "And it shall come to pass that everyone who is left of all the nations which came against Jerusalem shall go up from year to year to worship the King, the LORD of hosts, and to keep the Feast of Tabernacles." Does it make any sense that we, who follow God, would be expected to celebrate Tabernacles before the Cross, but not after the Cross, and then expected to celebrate it again after He returns?

- If Christ is the Word of God (John 1:14; Revelation 19:13) and He is the same yesterday, today, and forever (Hebrews 13:8), then how is it that the Word of God is not the same yesterday, today, and forever?

- If the Law has been done away with as many believe, by what standard will God judge man at the end of time?

- Why does Christianity as a whole acknowledge all of the Ten Commandments except the fourth one, the one concerning the Sabbath? This seems especially troubling since there is no Scriptural basis for the omission. Could it be that tradition is trumping the Commandment?

- A careful reading of the "New Covenant" prophesy in Jeremiah 31:31–33 makes it clear that this New Covenant is with the House of Judah and the House of Israel. How can Christians say that the New Covenant is for them and that it frees them from the burden [sic] of the Torah?

- In Deuteronomy 7:6, et al., God rather clearly designated Israel as His chosen people. What did that mean and why did He do that? Has that changed through the centuries? How does that make you feel as a Christian?

May I Ask a Favor?

May I ask a favor of you? I would love for you to leave a review on my Amazon page as your comments will assist others looking for information, and will assist me in the development of future books.

Simply go to:

www.amazon.com/dp/1492202800

Look for a button that reads "Create your own review" on the right side of the page and click the button to get started.

Thank you so very much.

God bless you!
Jerry.

Meet the Author

D r. Jerry Graham received a Master's Degree in Industrial Engineering from the University of Arkansas, and worked for Eastman Kodak for 25 years in various engineering and marketing positions.

His desire to serve God led him to Regent University in Virginia where he graduated with a Master of Divinity degree. He served as the Associate Pastor in a large charismatic church in Rhode Island, and has consulted with over 150 churches as a church growth consultant.

Jerry has had several articles published by national and international publications and for many years was a Contributing Editor of *Strategies for Today's Leader* magazine and served on the Editorial Board of the *Journal of Christian Coaching* for several years.

Jerry has a Ph.D. from Christian Leadership Seminary and a Doctor of Ministry degree from Fuller Theological Seminary with a focus in church growth.

He served as Administrator and then as Director of Equipping and Assimilation for New Life Christian

Fellowship, a church with multiple satellite congregations serving South Hampton Roads, Virginia. He also served as the Executive Director of Vanguard Ministries, an apostolic network of churches and ministries, and is now self-employed as a lifestyle coach and church/business consultant. Jerry is a Lifeforming Leadership Coaching (formerly known as Transformational Leadership Coaching) Professional Certified Coach and Coach Trainer.

He and his wife, Sharon, also operate a highly successful home-based business assisting others to achieve health and financial stability.

NOTES:

NOTES:

28039768R00049

Made in the USA
Charleston, SC
30 March 2014